Many Kinds of Families

by Linda Yoshizawa

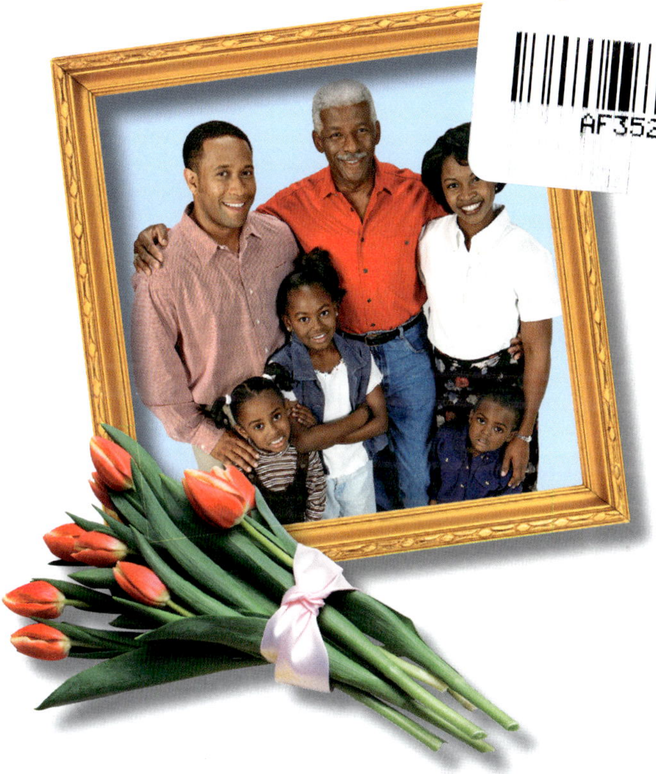

Scott Foresman
is an imprint of

PEARSON

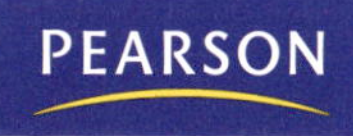

Glenview, Illinois • Boston, Massachusetts • Mesa, Arizona
Shoreview, Minnesota • Upper Saddle River, New Jersey

ISBN 13: 978-0-328-39298-8
ISBN 10:   0-328-39298-7

No family is just like mine.

Is one of these families like yours?

Many families have pets.

My family has a dog.

I said, "Let's walk our pup."

4

Many families like to have fun.

My family plays run and catch.

Dad said, "I can make you

laugh."

Many families shop together.
My family shops for food.
We put good things in bags.

Many families play games.
My family likes soccer.
I want to kick the ball.

No family is just like mine.
Is one of these families like yours?